LIGHT BULB
JOKES

By Jeffrey Armstrong

Carmel Bay Publishing Group

Text and cover design by Chris Shugart.

ISBN: 1-88353532-02-7

Carmel Bay Publishing Group
Box 222706, Carmel, CA 93922

Made in USA

The first light bulb joke dates back to 1864. It didn't catch on, since the light bulb hadn't been invented yet. By 1879, when Thomas Alva Edison finally did get around to inventing the light bulb, everybody had forgotten the joke.

That's why it's not included in this collection.

Also, it wasn't very funny.

How many New Yorkers does it take to change a light bulb?

None of your
goddam business!

How many New Yorkers who have moved to California does it take to change a light bulb?

None of your goddam business! Have a nice day.

3

How many people from New Jersey does it take to change a light bulb?

Three. One to change it, one to be a witness, and one to kill the witness.

How many Jehova's Witnesses does it take to change a light bulb?

Two, but it has to be your
front-porch light.

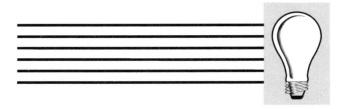

5

How many Teamsters does it take to change a light bulb?

Twenty-four, with triple pay for overtime. You got a problem with that, buddy?

6

How many Californians does it take to screw in a light bulb?

None. Californians don't screw in light bulbs, they screw in hot tubs.

How many Oregonians does it take to change a light bulb?

Five.
One to change the bulb
and four to chase away the
Californians who've come
to share the experience.

How many L.A. cops does it take to change a light bulb?

It depends on how much
the light bulb resists.

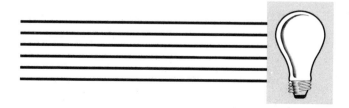

9

How many Democrats does it take to change a light bulb?

They can't change one,
because everyone keeps
turning in different
directions.

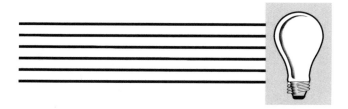

10

How many Republicans does it take to screw in a light bulb?

All of them.
One holds the bulb while
the rest screw the world.

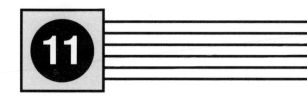

11

How many landlords does it take to change a light bulb?

Are you kidding?

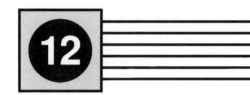

How many Jewish
mothers does it take to
change a light bulb?

Don't ask.

I'll just sit here in the dark.

13

How many Zen Buddhists does it take to change a light bulb?

Two.
One to, and one not to.

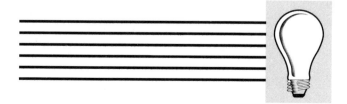

14

How many rock
musicians does it take
to change a light bulb?

Forty-seven.
One to perform the
act and forty-six to be
on the guest list.

15

How many Irishmen
does it take to change
a light bulb?

Six.
One to hold the light bulb
and five to drink until the
room starts spinning.

16

How many Dadaists
does it take to change a
light bulb?

Three.
One to change the
bulb and two to fill the
bathtub with brightly
colored power tools.

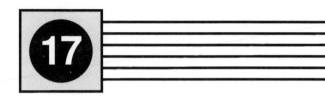

How many surrealists does it take to change a light bulb?

Fish!

How many Marxists does it take to change a light bulb?

None are needed.
Each light bulb contains
the seed of its own
revolution.

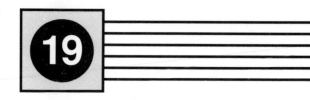

19

How many mystery writers does it take to screw in a light bulb?

Two.
One to turn it most
of the way, and the other
to give it the final twist.

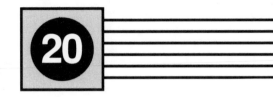

20

How many New-Age thinkers does it take to change a light bulb?

At least four.
One to change it, one
for support, and two to
share the experience.

How many Born-again Christians does it take to change a light bulb?

None.
They've already seen
the light.

22

How many Feminists does it take to screw in a light bulb?

That's not funny!

How many swingers
does it take to screw in
a light bulb?

Is that a regular bulb
or a three-way bulb?

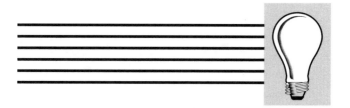

24

How many politicians does it take to screw in a light bulb?

Only one,
but it has to be in a ceiling
socket, because politicians
always screw up.

25

How many lawyers
does it take to screw
in a light bulb?

That'll be one hundred dollars, what's your second question?

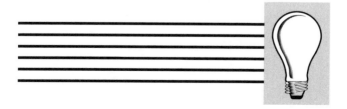

How many Americans does it take to change a light bulb?

Isn't someone else
supposed to take care
of this?

27

How many computer programmers does it take to screw in a light bulb?

None.
That's a hardware problem.

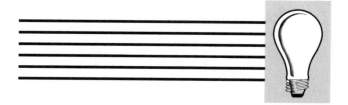

28

How many engineers
does it take to change
a light bulb?

Six.
One to change it
and five to write the
documentation.

29

How many chiropractors does it take to change a light bulb?

Only one. But it takes
twenty-five visits.

30

How many semanticists does it take to change a light bulb?

What do you mean by that?

31

How many Maoists
does it take to change
a light bulb?

According to official party records, none of our light bulbs has ever burned out. Tell me, who is spreading this vicious propaganda?

32

How many free-market economists does it take to change a light bulb?

None. It will eventually change itself according to the law of supply and demand.

33

How many plastic
surgeons does it take
to change a light bulb?

Three.
One to change it, one to
give a second opinion,
one to prepare for the
malpractice suit.

34

How many technical support representatives does it take to change a light bulb?

That's a good question.
Can I get back to you on
that later?

35

How many insurance agents does it take to change a light bulb?

Only one, but you never know when they'll burn out again, or whether you'll be able to afford new ones...Say, how many people in your family currently use light bulbs?

36

How many middle managers does it take to change a light bulb?

A feasibility study is being designed to evaluate market response and the cost-effectiveness of changing light bulbs.

37

How many EST trainees
does it take to change a
light bulb?

All of them, one at a time,
as the trainer tells them
what screw-ups they are.

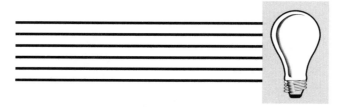

38

How many Texas he-men
does it take to change a
light bulb?

None! Hell, son,
that's women's work.

39

How many H. Ross Perot followers does it take to change a light bulb?

They can't change
one-but they have the
names of millions of
people who want to.

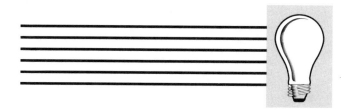

40

How many Hollywood agents does it take to change a light bulb?

Just one.
Trust me on this-it's a
standard contract.

41

How many auto
mechanics does it take
to change a light bulb?

Only one. But it looks like
we need to replace the
socket too-and we better
take a look at the wiring
while we're in there...
You want it by when?

42

How many Catholic priests does it take to change a light bulb?

Two.

One to screw it in, and the other to hear his confession.

43

How many grandmothers does it take to change a light bulb?

Three.
One to change it and two
to reminisce about how
nice the old one was.

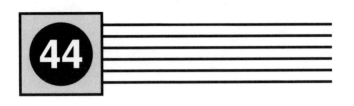

How many honest politicians does it take to change a light bulb?

Both of them.

45

How many doctors
does it take to change
a light bulb?

That depends.
Does the bulb have
medical insurance?

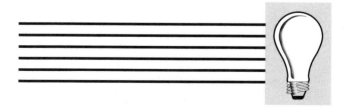

46

How many college football players does it take to change a light bulb?

Only one, and he gets
three credits for it.

47

How many WASPs
does it take to change
a light bulb?

Three.
One to change the bulb,
one to mix the martinis,
and one to turn on the
Princeton-Yale game.

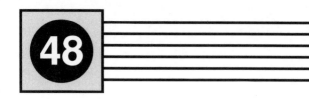

48

How many anorexics
does it take to change
a light bulb?

Only one, so long as it's not in the refrigerator.

49

How many nuclear
engineers does it take
to change a light bulb?

That's a moot question. According to our calculations, there's only a one-in-a-million chance of a light bulb ever burning out.

How many
environmentalists
does it take to change
a light bulb?

None. There could be a very tiny bug that lives inside light bulb sockets that just might be on the endangered species list.

51

How many Ku Klux Klan members does it take to change a light bulb?

None. They prefer to
work in the dark.

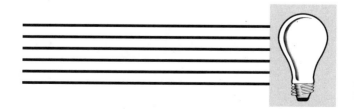

52

How many tabloid reporters does it take to change a light bulb?

None.
Unless it's at Graceland,
Buckingham Palace, or
the Kennedy compound.

53

How many lobbyists
does it take to change
a light bulb?

None. But by offering an all-expenses-paid trip to the Bahamas they can get a Congressman to do it.

54

How many accountants
does it take to change a
light bulb?

Only one, but first you
have to provide a receipt
for the old bulb.

55

How many punk-rockers
does it take to change a
light bulb?

Two.

One to break the new one
and one to eat the old one.

56

How many divorced husbands does it take to screw in a light bulb?

None.
The light-sockets went
along with the house.

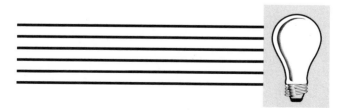

57

How many heavy-metal
fans does it take to
change a light bulb?

What did you say?

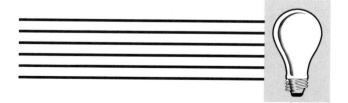

58

How many farmers
does it take to change
a light bulb?

None. They get a subsidy
for not changing them.

59

How many socialists
does it take to change
a light bulb?

All of them are supposed
to, but none of them does.

How many theoretical physicists does it take to change a light bulb?

Three.
One to change it, one to
say it may or may not be
changed, and one to say
there's no way to prove
it has been changed.

61

How many egotists
does it take to change
a light bulb?

Only one.
He holds the bulb, while
the whole world revolves
around him.

62

How many gorillas
does it take to screw
in a light bulb?

Only one, but it sure takes a lot of light bulbs.

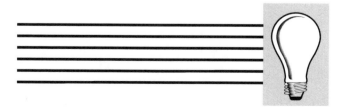

63

How many college professors does it take to change a light bulb?

Only one, but he publishes three papers about it and the bulb is actually changed by his graduate assistant.

64

How many total-immersion Baptists does it take to change a light bulb?

None. Whenever they try,
they get electrocuted.

65

How many ACLU lawyers does it take to change a light bulb?

Three.
One to change it, one
to hold the ladder, one to
file suit alleging wattage
discrimination.

66

How many corporate
executives does it take
to change a light bulb?

Three.
One to identify the
problem, one to order
the bulb, and one to
call maintenance.

67

How many graduate students does it take to change a light bulb?

Only one, but it may take
as long as five years.

68

How many "real men" does it take to screw in a light bulb?

None.
"Real men" aren't afraid
of the dark.

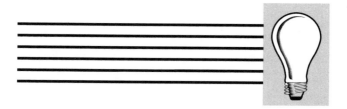

69

How many "real women" does it take to change a light bulb?

None,
"real women" would
have plenty of "real men"
around to do it for them.

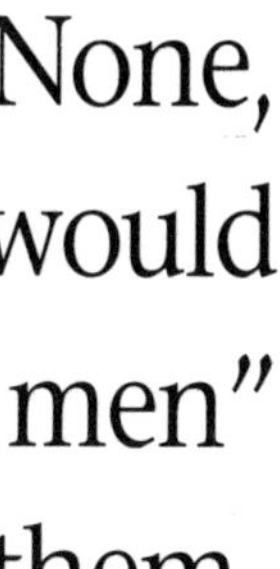

70

How many jugglers
does it take to change
a light bulb?

Only one, but it takes at
least three light bulbs.

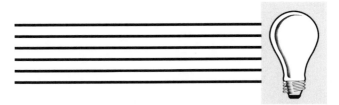

71

How many police detectives does it take to screw in a light bulb?

None. They wait for
it to turn itself in.

72

How many nuclear power plant workers does it take to change a light bulb?

Seven.
One to install the new
bulb, and six to figure
out what to do with the
old one for the next ten
thousand years.

73

How many Military leaders does it take to change a light bulb?

1,000,001.
One to destroy the old
bulb and a million to
rebuild civilization to the
point where they have
light bulbs again.

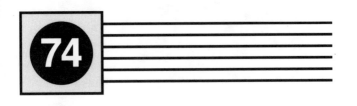

How many civil servants does it take to change a light bulb?

Forty-five.
One to change the bulb
and forty-four to handle
the paperwork.

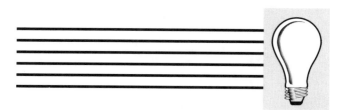

75

How many psychologists does it take to change a light bulb?

Only one, but the bulb has to be willing to change.

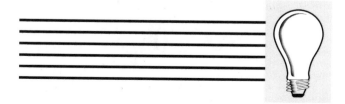

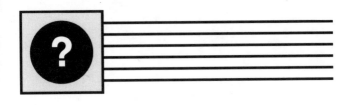

If you'd like to see your
own favorite light bulb
joke in our next book,
send it to:

Light Bulb
Box 222706
Carmel, CA 93922
FAX (408) 375-5137
Attn: Nick Tesla